KT-438-472

Sing a Song of Sixpence

Chosen by Vince Cross

Illustrated by Nick Sharratt

Northamptonshire
Libraries

J

OXFORD UNIVERSITY PRESS

Sing a song of sixpence

Sing a song of sixpence,
A pocket full of rye;
Four and twenty blackbirds,
Baked in a pie.

When the pie was opened,
The birds began to sing,
Wasn't that a dainty dish,
To set before the king?

The king was in his counting-house,
Counting out his money;
The queen was in the parlour,
Eating bread and honey.

The maid was in the garden,
Hanging out the clothes,
When down came a blackbird
And pecked off her nose.

Hector Protector

Hector Protector was dressed all in green;
Hector Protector was sent to the queen.
The queen did not like him,
No more did the king;
So Hector Protector was sent back again.

Two birds

There were two birds sat on a stone,
Fa la la la lal de;
One flew away, and then there was one,
Fa la la la lal de;
The other flew after, and then there was none,
Fa la la la lal de;
And so the poor stone was left all alone,
Fa la la la lal de.

Six little mice

Six little mice sat down to spin;
Pussy passed by and she peeped in.
'What are you doing, my little men?'
'Weaving coats for gentlemen.'
'Shall I come in and cut off your threads?'
'No, no, Mistress Pussy, you'd bite off our heads.'
'Oh no, I'll not; I'll help you to spin.'
'That may be so, but you don't come in!'

HOUSE OF
MOUSE

GARMENT
MAKERS

Pop goes the weasel

Up and down the City Road,
In and out the Eagle,
That's the way the money goes,
Pop goes the weasel!

Half a pound of tuppenny rice,
Half a pound of treacle,
Mix it up and make it nice,
Pop goes the weasel!

Every night when I go out
The monkey's on the table;
Take a stick and knock it off,
Pop goes the weasel!

Daffy-Down-Dilly

Daffy-Down-Dilly is new come to town,
With a yellow petticoat, and a green gown.

Sing, sing

Sing, sing,
What shall I sing?
The cat's run away
With the pudding string!
Do, do,
What shall I do?
The cat's run away with the pudding too!

Three little kittens

Three little kittens, they lost their mittens,
So they began to cry,
'Oh, mother dear, come here, come here,
For we have lost our mittens.'
'Lost your mittens? You naughty kittens,
Then you shall have no pie.'
'Miaou, Miaou. We shall have no pie.'

Three little kittens, they found their mittens,
So they began to cry,
'Oh, mother dear, come here, come here,
For we have found our mittens.'
'Found your mittens? You good little kittens,
Now you shall have some pie.'
'Prrrr! Prrrr! Now we shall have some pie.'

Peter Piper

Peter Piper picked a peck of pickled pepper;
A peck of pickled pepper Peter Piper picked.
If Peter Piper picked a peck of pickled pepper,
Where's the peck of pickled pepper Peter Piper
picked?

Little husband

I had a little husband;
No bigger than my thumb;
I put him in a pint pot
And there I bade him drum.
I gave him some garters
To garter up his hose,
And a little silk handkerchief
To wipe his pretty nose.

Polly put the kettle on

Polly put the kettle on,
Polly put the kettle on,
Polly put the kettle on,
We'll all have tea.

Sukey take it off again,
Sukey take it off again,
Sukey take it off again,
They've all gone away.

Tweedledum and Tweedledee

Tweedledum and Tweedledee
Agreed to have a battle,
For Tweedledum said Tweedledee
Had spoiled his nice new rattle.
Just then flew by a monstrous crow
As big as a tar-barrel,
Which frightened both the heroes so,
They quite forgot their quarrel.

See-saw

See-saw, Margery Daw,
Johnny shall have a new master;
He shall have but a penny a day,
Because he can't work any faster.

Jumping Joan

Here am I,
Little Jumping Joan;
When nobody's with me
I'm all alone.

Davy Dumpling

Davy Davy Dumpling,
Boil him in the pot;
Sugar him and butter him,
And eat him while he's hot.

Lucy Locket

Lucy Locket lost her pocket,
Kitty Fisher found it;
Not a penny was there in it,
Only ribbon round it.

Mother Shuttle

Old Mother Shuttle
Lived in a coal-scuttle
Along with her dog and her cat;
What they ate I can't tell,
But 'tis known very well
That not one of the party was fat.

Old Mother Shuttle
Scoured out her coal-scuttle,
And washed both her dog and her cat;
The cat scratched her nose,
So they came to hard blows,
And who was the gainer by that?

Lavender's blue

Lavender's blue, dilly, dilly,
Lavender's green;
When I am king, dilly, dilly,
You shall be queen.

Call up your men, dilly, dilly,
Set them to work,
Some to the plough, dilly, dilly,
Some to the cart.

Some to make hay, dilly, dilly,
Some to cut corn,
While you and I, dilly, dilly,
Keep ourselves warm.

Lavender's green, dilly, dilly,
Lavender's blue;
If you'll love me, dilly, dilly,
I will love you.

Elsie Marley

Elsie Marley is grown so fine,
She won't get up to feed the swine,
But lies in bed till eight or nine.
Lazy Elsie Marley.

Rub-a-dub-dub

Rub-a-dub-dub,
Three men in a tub,
And how do you think they got there?
The butcher, the baker,
The candlestick-maker,
They all jumped out of a rotten potato,
'Twas enough to make a man stare.

Bobby Shaftoe

Bobby Shaftoe's gone to sea,
Silver buckles at his knee;
He'll come back and marry me,
Bonny Bobby Shaftoe.

Bobby Shaftoe's bright and fair,
Combing down his yellow hair,
He's my ain for evermair,
Bonny Bobby Shaftoe.

Bobby Shaftoe's tall and slim,
He's always dressed so neat and trim,
The ladies they all keek at him,
Bonny Bobby Shaftoe.

Bobby Shaftoe's getten a bairn
For to dandle in his arm;
In his arm and on his knee,
Bobby Shaftoe loves me.

Cock a doodle doo

Cock a doodle doo!
My dame has lost her shoe,
My master's lost his fiddling stick,
And knows not what to do.

Cock a doodle doo!
What is my dame to do?
Till master finds his fiddling stick
She'll dance without her shoe.

Cock a doodle doo!
My dame has found her shoe,
And master's found his fiddling stick,
Sing doodle doodle doo.

Cock a doodle doo!
My dame will dance with you,
While master fiddles his fiddling stick
For dame and doodle doo.

A frog he would a-wooing go

A frog he would a-wooing go,
Heigh ho! says Rowley,
A frog he would a-wooing go
Whether his mother would let him or no.
With a rowley, powley, gammon and spinach,
Heigh ho! says Anthony Rowley.

Then off he set, in his opera hat,
And on the way he met a rat.

Together they came to the mouse's hall,
And there they did both knock and call.

But while they were all a-merry-making,
A cat and her kittens came tumbling in.

The cat she seized the rat by the crown,
And the kittens they pulled the little mouse down.

This put Mister Frog in a terrible fright,
He took up his hat and he wished them good-night.

Mister Frog ran home and was crossing a brook,
When a lily-white duck came and gobbled him up.

So that was the end of the one, two, three,
Heigh ho! says Rowley,
So that was the end of the one, two, three,
The rat and the mouse and the little frogg-ee.
With a rowley, powley, gammon and spinach,
Heigh ho! says Anthony Rowley.

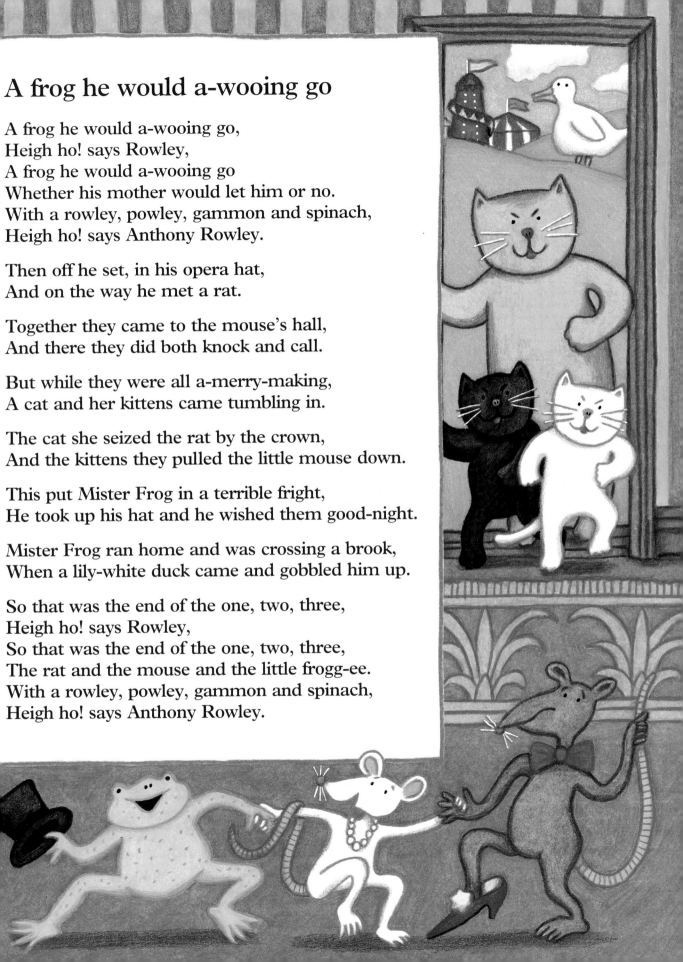

Oh dear, what can the matter be?

Oh dear, what can the matter be?
Dear, dear, what can the matter be?
Oh dear, what can the matter be?
Johnny's so long at the fair.

He promised he'd buy me a fairing should please me,
And then for a kiss, oh! he vowed he would tease me,
He promised he'd bring me a bunch of blue ribbons
To tie up my bonny brown hair.

He promised he'd bring me a basket of posies,
A garland of lilies, a garland of roses,
A little straw hat, to set off the blue ribbons
That tie up my bonny brown hair.

Feathers

Cackle, cackle, Mother Goose,
Have you any feathers loose?
Truly have I, pretty fellow,
Half enough to fill a pillow.
Here are quills, take one or two,
And down to make a bed for you.

Aiken Drum

There was a man lived in the moon,
    lived in the moon, lived in the moon,
There was a man lived in the moon,
    and his name was Aiken Drum;
And he played upon a ladle, a ladle, a ladle,
And he played upon a ladle,
And his name was Aiken Drum.

And his hat was made of good cream cheese,
    good cream cheese, good cream cheese,
And his hat was made of good cream cheese,
And his name was Aiken Drum.

And his coat was made of good roast beef,
    good roast beef, good roast beef,
And his coat was made of good roast beef,
And his name was Aiken Drum.

And his buttons were made of penny loaves,
    penny loaves, penny loaves,
And his buttons were made of penny loaves,
And his name was Aiken Drum.

His waistcoat was made of crust of pies,
    crust of pies, crust of pies,
His waistcoat was made of crust of pies,
And his name was Aiken Drum.